النهاية

The End

Arabic
Reading Heroes

 GET IT ON
Google Play

 Download on the
App Store

https://play.google.com/store/apps/details?id=app.readingheroe.readingheroes

https://apps.apple.com/gb/app/arabic-reading-heroes/id1523648270

يرقة

Yaa

ياء

وطواط

Wow

واو

هدهد

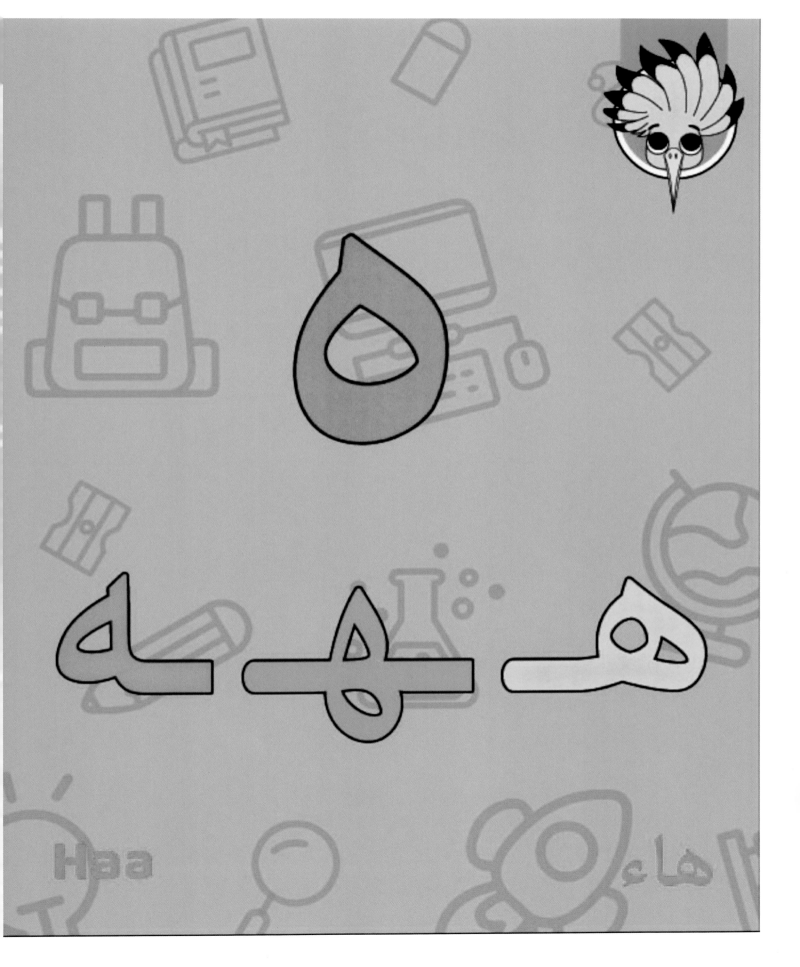

ه ـه ـهـ هـ

Haa

نمر

ن ـن ـنـ نـ

نون

Noon

ماعز

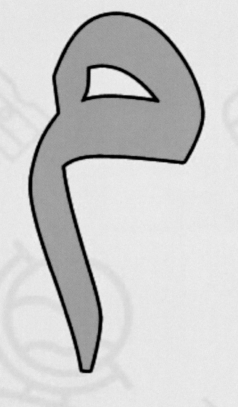

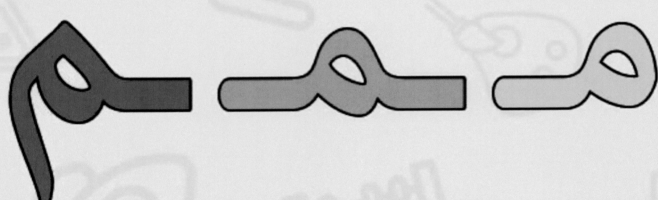

Meem

ميم

لقلق

Lam

لام

كلب

Kaf

كاف

قرد

قاف

Qaf

فيل

Faa

فاء

غوريلا

Ghayn

غين

عصفور

Ayn

عين

ظبي

ظ

ظـ ـظـ ـظ

Zah

ظاء

طاووس

Tah

طاء

ضفدع

ض ضـ ـضـ ـض

ضاد

Dhad

شِبْل

ش ـشـ ـشـ ـش

Sheen

شين

سمكة

س

سـ ـسـ ـس

Seen

سين

زرافة

Zay

زاي

راكون

ر
رَ

Raa

راء

ذِئْب

Thal

ذال

دب

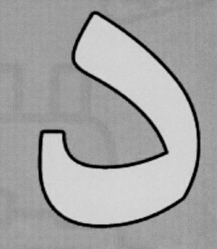

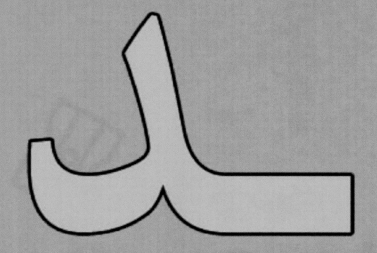

Dal

دال

خروف

خاء

Khaa

حصان

Haa

حاء

جمل

Jeem

جيم

ثعلب

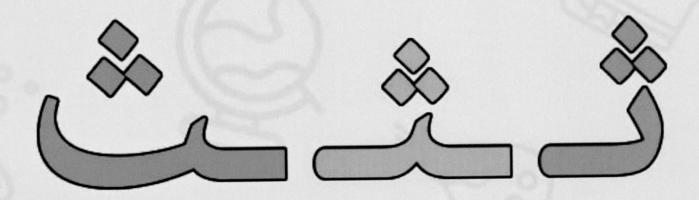

ثاء

Thaa

تنين

Taa

تاء

بطة

Baa

أرنب

Alef

الف

Made in the USA
Monee, IL
09 September 2022